No Laughs to Know Laughs

How To Be Funny To Make More Money

Rory Vaden

07 08 09 HH 5 4 3 2 1

First Edition

Printed in the United States of America

ISBN 10: 0-87197-535-1

ISBN 13: 978-0-87197-535-5

$14.95 - U.S. Funds

Every effort has been made to make this book as accurate as possible. However, there may be mistakes either typographical and/or in content. Therefore this text should be used only as a general guide and not as the ultimate source of information.

Neither the author nor the publisher make any claims of ownership regarding the quotes/sayings. The quotes used in this edition were used to illustrate the author's point of view.

Dedication

This book is dedicated to:

Bill, Jerry, and Ellen for inspiring me to be funny.
Eric, Dave, and Darren for teaching me how.
Tessie, Kevin, and Randy for believing me to be.

Thank you God for
making me have to work so hard to find my funny
so that I could help others begin to find theirs.

No Laughs to Know Laughs
How To Be Funny
To Make More Money

Contents

Appendix

 # Acknowledgements

Eric Chester, CSP, CPAE; Dave Avrin; Darren LaCroix, 2001 World Champion of Public Speaking (WCPS); Craig Valentine, MBA, 1999 WCPS; Mark Scharenbroich, CSP, CPAE; Mark Sanborn, CSP, CPAE; Eddie Brill; Dan Moore, MBA; Lee Mc-Croskey; Roger Seip; Brad Montgomery, CSP; David Glickman, CSP; Ed Tate, 2000 WCPS; David Brooks, 1990 WCPS; Jim Key, 2003 WCPS; Scott Friedman, CSP; and Tim Gard, CSP.

Acknowledgements to those I have not met: Bill Cosby, Jerry Seinfeld, Ellen DeGeneres, Mort Utley, Robin Williams, Mitch Hedberg, Brian Regan, Michael Jr., Josh Blue, Gene Perret, Melvin Helitzer, Judy Carter, Dane Cook, Aries Spears, George Lopez, and Michael Kerr.

The above listed people truly are the ones who are responsible for providing most of the information in this book; I'm only responsible for packaging it in this way.

Introduction

As a kid I learned so much from *The Volume Library*. *The Volume Library* was a set of encyclopedia-type reference books that my mom bought that helped me with 40 different school subjects, I loved it growing up because it had math, and science, and naked people.

Although money was tight for us, my mom always tried to buy my brother and me whatever we wanted. I was raised by a single mother who sold Mary Kay, which means that I know more about makeup than I do about cars. I know that for women, every morning goes like this: wash, toner, moisturizer, foundation, wrinkle-free eye cream, base eye shadow, dark eye shadow, blush, eyeliner, mascara, lip liner, and lipstick.

As fate would have it, I was recruited for The Southwestern Company's direct sales internship program when I was 18 years old. I earned almost $200,000 in my four summers while in college by selling the Volume Library to families across the country.

All of that is really just a nice way of saying, "I grew up to be a door-to-door salesman." That's right I was the most hated of all professions; I was like the human version of email spam. I'll put it to you this way; I bugged telemarketers when they were eating dinner. In my defense though, I never wanted to go door-to-door. I was a perfectly normal child; I wanted to sell Mary Kay.

One of the worst days of my life came when I was working on the book-field during my first summer in Montgomery, AL. It was about three in the afternoon and I hadn't been in a door all morning. My pink Barbie bike (the kind with the frillies coming out of the handle bars) that I had been riding around on had gotten a flat tire earlier that morning. So ironically, I was now a peddler who was on foot.

Although it had been raining water droplets that were about the size of small ornaments for about an hour, it was still about 90 degrees because of the humidity. My hair was slopping in my face, my sample books were soaked, and I trudged my prune-wrinkled feet through the puddles as I carried my negative attitude up to the door of my next feeble frustrating failure.

If You Can Make Someone Laugh, It is Like Their Personal Door Opening To You.

I knocked on the door and when the dad answered I accidentally said something that would change my perspective for the rest of my life. He answered, and out of some sort of irreverent apathy I said, "Hi, my name is Rory, and I'm not interested…oh wait, that's your line." And then the weirdest thing unfolded in front of me. The man burst out laughing! Then what happened next was even more unexpected. He opened the door and invited me in. It was at that very moment that I drew this incredibly powerful insight:

If you can make someone laugh, it is like their personal door opening to you.

That was the first time in my life that I had ever really made someone laugh. Not only was I able to get in the door and establish a wonderful connection with the man, but I also got the most sensational feeling out of making him laugh.

I was familiar with the saying that The Southwestern Company had that said: "Be funny; make money," but I never paid much attention to it because I was not naturally a funny person. However, once I became consciously aware of the benefits of making people laugh I began to pay close attention to what caused people to laugh.

In fact, I was enamored with why some people were always so funny while other people (such as myself) never seemed to get people laughing. Another way of saying it is that I did not want to spend the rest of my life being one of those people who could get no laughs. As a result, I set out on the journey to figure out how I could get to know laughs.

For the rest of my career at Southwestern I was never able to pinpoint what really caused people to laugh. However, since I was giving the exact same sales presentation thousands and thousands of times, I was able to mentally note when I would make people laugh on accident, and then I would start to re-create those lines on purpose in later sales presentations. By the end of my fourth summer my sales talk was more like a stand up comedy routine than a product pitch. You may have guessed by now that not only did I begin to enjoy my job a lot more, but I began to sell a lot more books!

Naturally my interest in humor only fueled my fire to pursue my childhood dream, which was becoming a professional speaker. As a young speaker I quickly realized that if I was going to be one of the best in the world that I would have to learn to become funny, which, for me at the time, was a daunting task. I began to study and I watched how some of the greatest speakers in history used humor to pierce into the most skeptical minds, to warm the coldest souls, and to lift the most discouraged hearts.

My whole life people had insisted that "you are either born funny or you are not," but by this time I refused to accept it. I just wasn't prepared to sit around subject to the nature of my DNA. So I became obsessed with humor and what actually caused people to laugh.

Today, as the co-founder of **Success Starts Now!**™ motivational sales training conferences, I am able to speak to thousands of sales professionals every year all across the globe. It didn't take me long to figure out that, like me, most people wish that they could be funnier! An even more important realization I had is that everyone likes people who are funny.

In sales, if people like you then they will buy from you, and making someone laugh is the fastest way to make someone begin to like you.

In my career as a professional speaker I was able to take classes, watch films, read books, and learn the secrets of humor from some of the funniest people in the world. Although many of them are professional speakers or comedians, they are quoted in this book because the same rules that apply to stand up comedy also apply to sales presentations.

I also noticed that most salespeople tend to do a certain amount of public speaking and that most speakers tend to do a certain amount of sales. So in that way, this book is for both salespeople and speakers, because an audience is an audience whether it is one person or a thousand people.

Introduction

While I never set out to write a book on humor, I learned that there really aren't any books that go through step by step why a person laughs. I wrote this book for the average citizen who wants to be at least a little bit funnier. This book is not intended to make you Jerry Seinfeld, but it will take you through a very systematic approach to what psychologically causes a person to laugh. And I can promise you that as you read this book you will begin the process of becoming a funnier person—a process that I guarantee will continue for the rest of your life.

 In sales, if people like you then they will buy from you, and making someone laugh is the fastest way to make someone begin to like you.

Chapter One -
The Humor Rumor

What is "funny?" What makes the masses laugh? And most important, how can you get more laughs when you interact with or present to others?

> The only thing we CAN produce and tangibly measure is laughter.

First, realize that no standard unit of measurement for "funny" exists, and thus I'm not sure I can MAKE you funny. However, I can give you some guidelines to humor and some suggestions that have worked for others to get laughs.

So again, what exactly does being "funny" mean? Well, being funny really means being disciplined. It means taking the principles in this text and studying them, applying them, and trying them out over and over until you master them. Most of being funny directly relates to your willingness to be disciplined.

When it comes to being funny, the only thing we **CAN** produce and tangibly measure is laughter. Therefore, this book is really about producing laughter. So after we talk about why it's important to laugh, we will take a look at WHY we laugh. That is, what happens psychologically to cause a laugh to happen? Once you understand why people laugh, then we will talk about overcoming the fear of trying to be funny. Finally, at the end of this book,

I will show you practical step-by-step humor formulas that are guaranteed to get laughs in your presentation and your life.

The Popular Misconception

There are two types of people in this world: those who were born funny and those who were not…right? Wrong! Actually, there are four types of people in the world as they relate to humor. They are:

1. People who are not funny. Most people in the world are not funny, and will never be funny. These types of people (of which I was a former class member) live with the popular and disempowering misconception that "you are either born funny or you're not." One reason they believe this is because the next largest percentage of the world is…

2. People who are just naturally funny. These people are often referred to as "the life of the party," "the class clown," and the person that "everyone likes." Do you know someone like this? Of course you do! We all do. If you're like me (and I know I am) you probably envy these people. The interesting insight here is that many of these naturally funny people have no idea why they are funny. In that way, they contribute to that disempowering misconception that you are either born funny or you're not.

3. People who learned how to be funny. A very small percentage of the world that was born "not funny" has learned how to be funny. My hunch is that many of the funniest people in the world (big name comedians) are in this category. They have cracked the code and figured out that humor is less of a talent that you are blessed with and more of a skill you can learn and develop. However, almost none

of these people will share their secrets with us, because it is the equivalent of a magician letting us in on the truths behind his or her tricks.

4. People who have learned how to be funny...and how to share. Finally, an incredibly minute percentage of the world is people who were born "not funny," have learned how to be funny, and are willing to teach others how to be funny. Trust me when I tell you that I was not funny! As 2001 World Champion of Public Speaking Darren LaCroix says, "The first time my family ever laughed at me was when I told them I wanted to be a comedian." But I have learned how to be funny, and more important, I'm willing to share my secrets with you.

Where My Funny Came From

I started speaking professionally around the same time I began graduate school. Prior to that I had been in many different sales positions, and I noticed that in both speaking and selling, the biggest challenge was getting the audience to be willing to be open-minded to what I was saying.

 Humor is, without a doubt, a very structured discipline with laws that govern it and apply always.

When I started professional speaking, my first audiences were large groups of high school students. So when I went from sales to professional speaking, I realized that if was going to really impact kids then I would have to find some way to hold their attention—I'd have to learn how to make them laugh. That need spurred a two-year in-depth study where I became obsessed with comedy and making people laugh. I studied hundreds of speakers/comedians, read dozens of books, listened to hours and hours of learning CDs, and even flew around the country on occasion to take courses on humor. It was only a matter of time before I realized the value of developing this skill so that I could utilize it in all aspects of my life.

What I discovered was that humor is, without a doubt, a very structured discipline with laws that govern it and apply always. I spent hours and hours meticulously studying the films of many of the best humorists in the world and learned so much. This book is a compilation of the best of what they taught me. And I've structured the information in such a way that even the most boring person can understand and benefit from it.

Why Make Em Laugh?

Before we get into our discussion of why people laugh, we need to identify some reasons why anyone would want to learn what it takes to make others laugh. We need to spend a few moments on the "Why," because if you know why you're trying to do something, you'll figure out the "How."

For most people, myself included, the real reason why we want to learn how to be funny is because we like people who are funny, and we want to be liked. Admit it…whenever you meet someone who is particularly funny, not only do you like the person, but you also secretly think to yourself, "Wow, I wish I was that funny."

The simple fact is that we are attracted to people who make us laugh. Whether we're trying to make new friends or trying to get a date, we all want to be around people who make us laugh and bring enjoyment to our lives.

And it doesn't matter whether you're making a sales presentation to a married couple or delivering a speech in front of 1,000 people, getting an audience to laugh is one of the best feelings in the world—and it's completely legal. Hearing those laughs is actually a lot like a drug, because once you experience the joy of making people laugh, you want those laughs more and more. It's an addicting experience.

When presenting in any way, shape, or form, think of humor like an E.K.G. If you were to graph your audience's attention span (or prospect, if you're selling), making the y-axis their attention and the x-axis their time, you would find that usually your audience's enjoyment looks something like this:

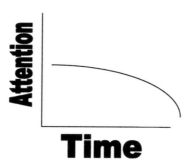

As shown here, you can see that for the average adult, their attention will be the highest in the beginning of any presentation. And because we are so accustomed to media happening in short spurts, our attention will fade off as time goes on even if we are listening to a presenter that is very good. Eventually the audience's attention span will flat line, which is essentially death to any presenter.

Humor, however, is a tool you can use to pique the audience's interest. Humor brings attention and focus back to what you are saying and helps to make for a more enjoyable presentation for everyone. When you use humor, your audience's attention span looks more like this:

Just as the lines rise and fall as a sign of a healthy heart on an E.K.G., they are also the signs of a healthy presentation—one that is filled with humor and holding the audience's attention.

Another reason to consider adding humor to your presentation is that humor gives you additional credibility, regardless of whether you are a salesperson, a speaker, or a teacher. I once heard a great quote from a comedian whose name I can't remember, but it goes like this: "Humor is a lubricant for your message." When an audience or a prospect is laughing regularly, they have an easier time retaining your overall message.

In addition, the US Department of Bogus Statistics says that the general public will retain up to 50% more of the information you present if you do it in a humorous way (that's roughly one laugh every three to five minutes). Actually, I'm not sure what the exact percentage is, but numerous researchers have validated the claim that laughter helps people remember information, as well as provides phenomenal aerobic benefits for the body, such as lowering cholesterol, stress levels, etc.

I learned one of the most important lessons about humor while I was in college selling educational children's books door-to-door for five summers. The Southwestern Company, which I worked for, had a positive phrase that I used to repeat out loud between houses: "Be funny; make money."

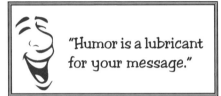

"Humor is a lubricant for your message."

In knocking on over 3,000 doors each summer, my sales presentation became a part of who I was. After a couple of summers I had acquired so many little jokes to insert into my sales demonstration that by my fourth summer I felt like I was doing a stand up comedy routine rather than a sales presentation. Not only was I having more fun, but so were my customers. And it was unbelievable what a little humor did for my sales. I went from making about $15,000 in sales my first summer to making almost $40,000 in sales my later summers. Realize that sales (and speaking, for that matter) is all about making people like you and trust you. And if you can make people laugh, they will open up their checkbooks, I promise.

One of the most famous stories in speaking comes from the founder of the National Speakers Association and former World Champion of Public Speaking, Cavett Robert. A young speaker once asked him, "Do I have to be funny to be a professional speaker?" Cavett responded, "No son, only if you want to be paid." This lesson holds true in a variety of professions: Be funny; make money.

Finally, you should be excited about learning to make people laugh simply because it is so much fun! Having just completed my MBA, I can vouch for the frustration and pain of studying topics that are tedious and boring. But humor is an absolute riot to learn about. So study hard!

Studying Humor

The first way to study humor is to watch good humor. After all, what can be more fun than that? Well, possibly going down a chocolate syrup slip and slide into a pool of whipped cream, but not really anything else. My favorite activity is to rent different stand up acts from my local video store. In fact, when I was in college and many of my friends were out getting wasted, I was home "studying." But for me, studying meant watching comedy. After you finish this book, you'll be able to watch comedy completely differently, analyzing and picking apart different punchlines.

Another fun part of studying humor is writing it. Few processes are as stimulating and challenging as trying to write jokes. While the idea of writing a joke may seem alien to you, by the end of this book you will have specific exercises you can do to develop your funny bone.

 Few processes are as stimulating and challenging as trying to write jokes.

One of the most enriching experiences is when you get to the point where you are going to perform your newly created humor. You'll feel a fabulous sense of anticipation in the moments leading up to your initial test of your comedic material. Whether you're going to an open mic, a Toastmaster club, or testing something out on a new prospect, performing humor is something that will get your nerves up and get you out of bed in the morning.

So, What is Laughter?

As Motivational Humorist Brad Montgomery says, "It is important to note that when we talk about generating laughter from an audience or a prospect we aren't necessarily talking about getting someone to fall out of their chair doubled over with laughter; in fact we aren't even always talking about that they laugh out loud at all." Very often, getting a chuckle from an audience or getting a prospect to think silently "oh, that was funny" is all we need to gain success.

Of course, it is always enjoyable to make people laugh so hard that they pee their pajamas. However, there are plenty of instances where an out loud laugh isn't necessary or may not even be appropriate, such as at a eulogy or during a very professional presentation. So realize that when we talk about "getting laughs," we are really talking about getting that little bell to ring in someone's head that says, "Ha, that was funny." Many times that simple little acknowledgement is all you need to go from losing the sale to making the sale, or from losing an audience to winning an audience. It's that simple realization that something is funny that brings about the little blip on the E.K.G. and re-awakens your audience.

By the way, in case you haven't realized it yet, the phrases "making a sale" and "winning the audience" are the same thing. All presentations are nothing more than sales pitches, and all sales calls are presentations. Many people are afraid to learn how to sell and even more are afraid to learn how to present, but make no mistake about it…all of life is some sort of a sales presentation. So from this point forward I will use the term "audience" as a word for both a sales prospect and a group of people. Now that we have added this little caveat about what laughter is, let's dive into what causes people to laugh.

Chapter Two -
Why Do
We Laugh?

There are a lot of funny people in the world, and there are a lot of terrific resources on the topic of humor. However, many of those resources neglect one key concept: "Why" people laugh. When I began studying humor I wasn't that interested in getting help to write good jokes. I really just wanted to learn "why" people laugh.

Once you are able to understand "why" people laugh then you never have to fear running out of funny material. Even better, you never have to rely solely on others to tell you what is funny and what isn't. The real empowering part of humor is having a tight grip on what causes a laugh to happen. If you know that, then you can find creative ways to reproduce those circumstances.

After years of study I have narrowed it down to the following ten basic reasons "why" people laugh. The information you are about to read will not only equip you to have more fun and bring in more business, but I guarantee that you will also begin the process of becoming a funnier person for the rest of your life.

1. Change in Expectation

The most popular way to make someone laugh is to create a change in expectation. Researchers say that the human mind thinks up to seven times faster than the average person talks. That means while you are speaking out loud to an audience, they are actually thinking ahead and subconsciously predicting what you are going to say next. As a result, subconsciously they are expecting to hear certain pieces of information from you.

Comedians understand this concept and they manipulate it to create laughter. They know that a laugh happens when the listener's mind hears something that is outside of its previous realm of expectation. As Darren LaCroix says, "We laugh when our minds are successfully tricked."

 "Learn to recognize when the audience is being led to believe something, know what they are expecting to hear, and give them ketchup when they are expecting a tomato."

For example, in his championship speech, Darren talks about a man who failed in his attempt to create a rocket that would reach the moon. He says, "Dr. Robert Goddard's first rocket took off in Auburn and landed…in Auburn." The laugh comes on the punch-line "in Auburn." By saying that the rocket took off in Auburn (and emphasizing the setup by pointing up at the stars), he tricks our minds to have a certain realm of expectation about what he is going to say next. Our minds think that if the rocket took off in Auburn then it must have landed in any number of other places, such as another state or another planet. He then tricks our minds when he says "in Auburn." That change in expectation is where the laugh happens.

Legendary comedian George Carlin said, "Think of a train on a track. The setup is leading the audience on a thought track, and then the laugh comes when you de-rail the thought train." For example, in a story I tell about the educational children's books my mom bought for me I use the following joke: "I loved the

Volume Library growing up because it had math, and science, and…naked people."

Here I created an expectation (set the audience on a thought track) of the different items that were contained in this book. When I say "math and science and…" the audience is expecting another type of school subject, like history or reading. Then the laugh comes when I say, "naked people."

Another famous comedian named Rory Vaden explains it this way, "Learn to recognize when the audience is being led to believe something, know what they are expecting to hear, and give them ketchup when they are expecting a tomato."

Here's an example of the "ketchup" versus "tomato" concept: In another one of my stories I talk about my worst day ever as a door-to-door salesperson. I describe all of the horrible events that happen to me that day and about the moment that I finally have a minute to talk with someone, the maid of one of my prospects. The story goes: "I say to her, 'I'm tired, it's raining, this guy yelled at me, a kid made fun of me, and it's my birthday.' She looked at me, and I'll never forget what this woman said…'No hablo Ingles!'"

When I originally wrote the line, I never intended it to be funny. But I talk for so long about how horrible this day was that when I finally meet this woman the audience expects her to be my saving grace. Giving the audience a "tomato" would've been having this woman tell me a pearl of wisdom or some kind of encouraging word. Giving the audience "ketchup" still meant giving her a line, but giving her one that was different than what they were expecting her to say.

2. Mental Exercise

People often laugh when you give them mental exercise. Why? Because our brains are constantly working and thinking ahead. We (meaning our brains) are always trying to piece ideas together. We try to organize information so that it makes sense to us. When we "get" or understand the punchline of a joke, it's because our mind has been able to assemble certain ideas or concepts together in a way that fits.

Knowing this fact about the human brain, we can talk in ways that allow our audience's mind to "get" things without even delivering punchlines. When they "get" it, they will usually laugh.

Coming up with new mental exercises for your audience can challenge your creativity, but when you come up with something good, your audience truly enjoys it. One of the best, spontaneous examples of a mental exercise that I have ever heard came from the 1999 World Champion of Public Speaking, Craig Valentine.

Craig was being introduced as he usually is before coming out on stage; however, unbeknownst to him, his introducer took all of his accomplishments and created a poem out of them. The audience was a group of Toastmasters who were very familiar with the World Championship of Public Speaking and what it takes to get there. Craig capitalized brilliantly on a once in a lifetime opportunity.

After the applause died down he simply stared at the crowd and said: *"The one thing Linda Shorter (name of his introducer) forgot to tell, the night before the championship I was scared as _____."*

He didn't even say the final rhyming word, but the audience laughed hysterically. With the setup that Craig's introducer provided (with her rhyming poem) the audience was able to "get it." The mind loves when that happens, which often results in a laugh.

I was first exposed to this mental exercise principle when I was breaking down an old film of my number one mentor's, Eric Chester. Eric was a youth speaker for over 20 years, and after becoming one of the best youth speakers in the world he turned his focus to speaking to companies. Today, Eric is a CPAE—recipient of the Council of Peers Award for Excellence, meaning that he has been inducted to the Speaker Hall of Fame. As a consultant and best-selling author and founder of his own company, Generation Why, Eric provides cutting edge insights into the minds of Generation Y.

One of Eric's old openings for youth audiences was when he created a list of questions by stringing together the names of many celebrities. For example:

★ Why did Mary have a little lamb?

★ Where does Tom Cruise?

★ What does Mariah Carey?

★ Is Martin Short?

★ Is Shelly Long?

Why did Chevy Chase Dan's Quayle through George's Bush right down Arsenio's Hall?

Was it because Robert's Redford was parked down Kirstie's Alley behind Roseanne's Barr?

This exercise continued for many minutes, and the kids loved it! Why? Because it was a mental exercise; our mind enjoys playing these little games, like listening for celebrity names and how they are used in this case.

When I watched Eric's opening, I realized that the names he used on the film wouldn't work for today's young audiences, but I was able to use his concept and create some similar bits for my speeches. I followed Eric's general idea and created a story that uses all the names of today's top celebrities, which is what I am famous for in front of teenage audiences. Here's an example: "I found it Ludacris that I had to pay 50 Cent for a 2 Pac of Eminem and some Black Eyed Peas."

One day while waiting for a flight, I had an idea to do the same with brand names of alcohol. Now I have a piece that kills in front of twenty-something-year-old college students. You'll find that some lines just lend themselves to humor such as, "You're knees can't slide on Molson Ice, but your Heini-ken."

All jokes are in some way an example of mental exercise. Knowing this principle will allow you to recognize opportunities where you can mentally challenge your audience members to fill in the gap or solve the puzzle.

3. Conjoining Unrelated Ideas

Mark Twain said, "Wit is the sudden marriage of two ideas which before their union, were not perceived to have any relation." That quote concisely summarizes why people laugh from conjoining unrelated ideas.

Using this concept is one of the simplest (although not always easiest) ways to get laughs. All you have to do is think of a funny reference and then think of a completely different reference that is polar opposite to the first.

One empowering and yet frustrating truth about humor writing is that it is a process. A great way of illustrating the process (and the principle of conjoining unrelated ideas) is to share with you how I stumbled upon one of my classic jokes.

A long time ago I heard that it was a good idea to keep a list of funny references. Simply put, you will often hear things that seem to be funny. It could be a reference to a thing, an idea, or even an object. Whatever it is, if you are paying attention, you'll notice potentially funny references everywhere. Well, I don't recall exactly when, but at some point in 2005 I either heard or read something about Amish people.

 "Wit is the sudden marriage of two ideas which before their union, were not perceived to have any relation."

While there's nothing inherently funny about Amish people— they are a good and kind community—I was able to recognize that "Amish" was a potential funny reference for the mainstream crowd and could possibly become a great joke. So I added "Amish" to my list of funny references, which hangs on a bulletin board above my desk. Then, a few weeks later, I was walking out of a bank and saw a huge red Hummer H2 in the parking lot. I thought to myself, "There's got to be something funny about a Hummer."

Again, I didn't know what was funny about a Hummer, but I recognized the potential for the word. So I added "Hummer" to my list.

A few months later, while I was working on a contest speech for an upcoming speech contest I was in, I decided that I needed a joke. The line in my speech was: "There was no way this family was going to have saved this money. There was a better chance of…" but I couldn't think of anything funny to say. I needed a punchline.

That's when I referred to my funny reference list and saw "Amish." Once I had "Amish," the word "Hummer" almost jumped off the page as its polar opposite. Thus one of my great lines was born: "There was no way this family was going to have saved this money. There was a better chance of an Amish family pulling up in a Hummer."

Okay, maybe it's not that funny to you as you read it on paper, but trust me, it's hilarious in front of an audience. Mark Twain figured out the power of polar opposites years ago, and it's a principle that still applies today. When you can find a way to join two seemingly unrelated ideas in a clever way, you will get a laugh.

4. Release of Stress

Chances are that if you walk into any comedy club on any given night, you will hear the comedians address some of the same topics: relationships, sex, work, bills, airports, traffic, kids, or parents. These topics are a natural fit for comedy, because people laugh as a way to deal with stress. So by bringing up things that are stressful for everyone, and things that everyone can relate to, a comedian has a free ride to easy laughs.

As comedian Dave Fitzgerald is famous for saying, "Comedians are just people who get paid to complain." This is so true, and you may have even noticed in your personal life that sometimes when you are stressed out, the smallest and stupidest things will cause you to laugh uncontrollably. That's simply your body's way or releasing any built up frustration that you have.

Therefore, any time you can write a joke that makes light of a stressful situation, you have the perfect opportunity to "connect" with your audience and make them laugh.

For example, here's a simple joke I've heard from a few different sources that illustrates my point. It's a joke that deals with the TSA, the airport security officials. This joke is effective because we've all been to the airport and have had to go through the long security lines operated by all those security guards. The joke goes like this:

"I was at the airport the other day. Boy, I hate those security lines. I figured something out while I was waiting at the carry-on screening. You know what TSA really stands for, right? Thousands Standing Around."

Especially in front of a room of sales managers or performers who travel a lot, this joke causes the place to erupt. Why? The joke exploits a pain point for people who travel frequently.

 "Comedians are just people who get paid to complain."

Of the hundreds of comedians I've studied, two exemplify this concept so masterfully that they have almost been able to make an entire career out of just this one idea. They are Jerry Seinfeld and Ellen DeGeneres. These two are absolutely brilliant in everything, from their writing and their delivery to their overall stage persona. And the one thing they do better than anyone is identify people's stress points.

In Jerry Seinfeld's HBO Special *I'm Telling You for the Last Time* (which I would argue is quite possibly the best 79 minutes of technical comedy ever strung together), he covers everything from cab drivers, to airports, to grocery stores, to childhood costumes, to old people, to relationships in a way that allows the audience to release their personal stresses.

Ellen DeGeneres wrote her phenomenal stand up *Here and Now* (which I've watched over 20 times) *entirely* on one point of stress for all of us: procrastination. On top of her seamless delivery and gestures, that comedy special is like rich creamy chocolate for your mind to indulge.

By now you might be thinking, "But I'm not Ellen DeGeneres or Jerry Seinfeld." Well, guess what? Neither am I…I'm not even close. However, just like everyone else, you deal with life's little stressors day in and day out. And if you know your audience (which you should), whether it's a single prospect or a large group of people, you are an expert on the things that frustrate them because you deal with them too.

So the next time you are seething with frustration or just straight pissed off with something that doesn't seem to make any sense, **WRITE IT DOWN!** You don't have to think of something funny in that moment; just jot down the circumstances and later you will probably think of something that was funny about the situation. Then, when you share that situation with your audience, you will "connect" with them and they will be able to appreciate where you are coming from.

5. An Exhale of Tension

For a beginning humorist, an exhale of tension in the room is a favorite way to get people laughing. This is a sister to reason number 4 of why people laugh, but it differs because it has to happen in the exact moment that tension fills the room.

Whether you are a speaker or a salesperson, you have undoubtedly noticed that there are moments in your presentation (and your overall life) that produce the dreaded "awkward tension." Here are some common things that cause tension in a room:

For Speakers:

★ Room distractions, such as a ringing cell phone, a crying baby, people coming in late, or broken technology

★ Accidental errors, such as mispronouncing a word, having a misspelling on a PowerPoint slide, or you totally forgetting what you were going to say

★ Bad jokes, such as ones nobody laughs at or ones that obviously offend most of the audience

For Salespeople (all the above as well as):

★ Initial Contact, when you first introduce yourself to someone

★ Price, when your prospect asks the question "how much does it cost?"

★ Close, when it's time for you to ask for the sale

These are just a few of the thousands of instances in our everyday communication that can produce a noticeable tension in the room. However, what you once considered awkward and avoided will now become your new best friend, because people laugh as an exhale of tension.

 Just as you often think of the perfect comeback line to a situation with a friend or co-worker weeks after the event, you will think of something funny to address these tense moments.

Think of it like this: Anytime one of these tension builders take place, it's like the room is taking a giant inhale along with you. During these moments, both you and your audience notice that something has happened, either because it was unplanned or just awkward in general. This is when you pop that tension or release it with a stock line.

The best way to handle these situations is to *acknowledge what has happened—what has just created the tension.* You don't even have to have a brilliant line; you just have to say what everyone else is thinking at that exact moment.

For example, say you are in front of a room leading a training session. You are telling a personal story, and right when you are at the most serious part of your story, someone's cell phone rings. Immediately, the room is filled with tension because every person in the room hears the ringing phone. In that situation you have to discipline yourself to first let the tension build, and then let the tension fester for two moments longer than feels comfortable. Then you can use one of a thousand stock lines, such as: "Hold my calls."

Once again, it may not seem funny reading it, but in that situation with all of that tension built, you are sure to get a laugh. When you deliver the line, it is an exhale of tension for the audience, and that is what creates the laugh.

This idea about using stock lines in moments of tension is something that industry professionals refer to as *planned spontaneity*. It's a powerful concept, because it appears to the audience that you have somehow thought of something to say very quickly to cause the laugh. In fact, many times the audience thinks, "Wow, (S)he's a genius!" when in fact you have a bunch of these lines memorized for different situations.

I hate to spoil the illusion for you, but I guarantee that every single polished comedian has various stock lines ready to go in the heat of the battle. This *planned spontaneity* is what gives comedians the appearance that they are naturally funny and able to think on their feet. While the great ones often do think on their feet, for the regular people like me, it's just another magic trick to make you think I'm more dynamic than I really am.

We will devote a significant amount of time to one form of *planned spontaneity*, called "saver lines," later in this book.

Although you may not be presenting on stage in front of large crowds, you will still likely encounter a number of situations during your presentations that generate tension. Pay attention to what these things are and write them down. Just as you often think of the perfect comeback line to a situation with a friend or co-worker weeks after the event, you will think of something funny to address these tense moments. And once you have something funny to say for those moments, you can use the line forever.

Just to help draw the connection a little more for those of you who work one-on-one with customers, here are some cheesy but effective examples I have used during tense moments when selling books door-to-door.

(While standing at the door): "Hi, Mr. Jones. My name is Rory and I'm not interested… Oh wait, that's you're line."

(When knocking after dark): "Hi, Mr. Jones. Sorry to stop by so late. I stopped by earlier but you must've been working too hard…want to trade jobs?"

(When asked, "Are you selling something?"): "What gave it away…my shoes?"

(When asked, "What are you selling?"): "Cages for your kids… I'm just here to take measurements."

(When asked, "What are you selling?"): "Nothing…today."

(When asking for money): "We take cash, checks, credit cards…dogs, cats, and kids."

(When asking for money): "We take all major credit cards except Chevron…and Enron."

(When asking for money): "We take cash…with two forms of ID."

(When the customer has a big dog): "Oh, has he been fed yet today? He doesn't like salespeople, does he?"

(When you encounter a disheveled mom): "Who is winning today…you or the kids?"

(When meeting someone): "Hi Sarah. Nice to meet you." (After Sarah asks, "What's your name?" I [a man] say): "Jennifer. Just kidding. My name is Rory."

I understand that you may never do door-to-door sales, but the point is for you to realize that you have certain tense situations that you repeatedly find yourself in. When you notice one, jot it down, and you will think of something funny later that you could've said. In fact, many times you can adapt something one of your co-workers comes up with in causal conversation. Remember, these lines don't have to be brilliant because all you're doing is breaking the tension. It is the exhale of tension that most often causes the laugh, not necessarily your perfect line.

By now everyone has heard that people like to do business with those they feel comfortable with. Laughter is one way to make people feel comfortable with you, and planned spontaneity is a great way to release tension.

6. Because Everyone Else is Laughing

One unexplainable phenomenon of laughter is that it is contagious. Nobody knows why; however, we have all been in that situation where you walk into a room and everyone is laughing,

One unexplainable phenomenon of laughter is that it is contagious.

and for some reason you can't help but start laughing yourself. Or have you ever had a time when you and a friend or family member laughed for 20 minutes over the same stupid thing? You couldn't stop laughing because the other person kept laughing, and it was a vicious cycle.

This is another dynamic that comedians and funny people understand, but the average person does not. And I have to admit that this is one of the few principles in this book that really only applies when you're presenting in front of a group. However, when you understand this concept you have an amazing advantage as a presenter. Why? Because you are going to do everything in your power to make sure that the room you are speaking in is set up for laughter.

Some comedians say that *setting* is as much as 33 percent responsible for how well a show goes. That means that you increase your chances of success dramatically just by controlling how a room is *set up*. That's huge!

<u>Lighting</u> - One simple thing you can often manipulate in your favor is how much lighting is focused on you. The more well lit you are, the better chance there is for the audience to see your facial expressions, and hence the funnier you will be.

<u>Space</u> - Another basic rule of room set up is to minimize the total space in a room. One of the best settings in the world for a comedy act is Comedy Works in Denver, Colorado. Comedians love to perform there because the ceiling is so low. When you have a lot of extra space in a room, whether from a vaulted ceiling or just a room that holds more people than are in attendance, the laughter dies out as it carries. In a tightly packed space the laughter is trapped and becomes louder, which causes people to laugh louder and for longer. So if you're presenting in a room

that is much too large for the actual attendance, see if the maintenance staff can help you pull out one of the floating walls to close off the space a little bit. Do whatever you can to eliminate unused space—you'll get more laughs.

Chair Proximity - The third physical characteristic of room set up that produces more laughter is chair proximity. The closer people are to one another, the more laughter it creates. There is something about being physically close to people that gives us a license to laugh more, plus the proximity allows for the maximum spread of the laughter disease. Also, it helps when people can see others laughing, so arranging the chairs in the room in some sort of a chevron or v-style allows for more laughter, because audience members will be able to see each other laughing and enjoying the show.

Stage Proximity - Stage proximity is also very important. The greater the distance between the speaking area and the audience, the less likely (s)he is to come across as funny. Always try to get the audience and the stage as close together as possible. Comedy is very intimate; the closer you are to your attendees, the better you will relate and the easier your energy will channel to them. In comedy clubs you will always see that the first row is right up on the stage, and they often have very small tables to ensure that people are packed together tightly.

Time of Day - Early in my speaking career I failed to recognize the importance "time of day" has on a presentation. As such, I agreed to speak to a group of college students at 8 a.m. on a Saturday. They promoted me to the students as a motivational humorist. Even at that point in my career I knew my material was funny and that it worked, but that day was the longest one hour presentation of my life. It taught me that an audience is not ready to laugh that early in the morning. Mid-afternoon and late night also tend to be poor laugh time periods. The prime time for laughter is from 10 a.m. to 1 p.m. and from 5 p.m. to 8 p.m. With that said, if a client wants to pay you to come in and do your thing at 8 a.m., then go ahead; but be sure to let your client know that the requested time frame typically doesn't work well for laughter.

If you're a salesperson, then be aware that most of your prospects are not going to be primed to laugh early in the morning or late in the evening. This is especially important for you to understand if you are doing some sort of a group sales presentation, such as to a room full of executives. Now, this doesn't mean you can't be effective as a persuader; it just means that you shouldn't expect too many laughs. If you are doing a sales presentation at one of these times I would recommend that you avoid any type of risky humor, such as new material or something that could be considered "over the top goofy."

Temperature - Room temperature is another physical part of setting that you want to have control over. Make sure the room is as cold as possible without it being distracting. Colder temperatures force the body to work hard to generate heat, and this forces you to stay awake and more alert. Speakers and comedians understand this and always try to keep the room cool. In fact, *The Tonight Show* has an exact temperature that the audience section is always sitting in just for this reason.

The Funny Aura - Also realize that **"setting"** is more than just the physical layout of a room; it is also what is happening in your audience's minds. And if you're good enough, you can create an "artificial setting" for your audience, called your "funny aura." This "aura" is why some of the great comedians can make something seem "funny" that audiences would probably never laugh at if someone else did.

Chapter Two - Why Do We Laugh?

While growing up, I had a favorite comedian: Bill Cosby. My favorite act of his was **Bill Cosby, Himself**. In that special, Cosby walks out on stage, and instead of turning to face the audience, he just slowly keeps walking all the way to the other side of the stage. Meanwhile the audience is going nuts with laughter. They loved it and thought it was hilarious, and I have to admit that I thought it was funny too.

What's funny about someone walking across a stage? Well, with Cosby, it's a change in expectation. The setup is walking out, and the audience always expects you to come right out and face them. The change in expectation happened exactly at center stage, as everyone figured out that he was going to keep walking; that's where the laugh happens.

Now if I walked out on stage and did what Cosby did, nobody would laugh; they would just think that I'm stupid. However, if you're Bill Cosby, it's an act of genius. He has such a strong "funny aura."

Developing a "funny aura" is simply a matter of creating a funny reputation. In fact, that "funny boy" in your group of friends who you are sometimes jealous of is often able to get laughs acting like an idiot whereas you might not. That's because of the law of the "funny aura." Judy Carter's book **Stand Up Comedy** is the best one out there on developing a reputation, or a stage persona. Obviously, being funny is the number one way to develop the "funny aura," but there are some other things that you and I can do to help us.

First, if you're a guest speaker you should always make the last line of your introduction funny. The easiest way to do this is to have your normal intro with all of your accomplishments (all the stuff nobody cares about anyway) and then have the last line somehow deflate the persona you just created. For example, one of the last lines in an intro I've used with youth audiences is, "Rory's track record of success dates all the way back to when he was young. (Setup) *At age 12 he became the youngest black belt in CO...*(punchline) to ever get beaten up by a girl." Find an accomplishment of yours that you can use to poke fun at yourself and arrange your introduction so it's the last line.

Additionally, to develop your "funny aura," you must always get a laugh within the first 30 seconds of your presentation. Why? Because that is the one and only moment where you have the full attention of every single audience member. At the start of any presentation, the audience's energy is always so vibrant and filled with positive expectation that if you can get a laugh right away they will label you as funny and will give you some free laughs along the way.

Think about it...great comedians always get a laugh in the first few seconds. Many times (as was the case for Cosby) they are able to get a laugh without saying anything. Pay attention to the opening comments professional speakers give. You will find that 99 percent of all speakers start with something lame like, "Thank you for being here...Let me tell you a joke." What a mistake! When you use an opener like that, you blow your one moment of heightened audience anticipation. Second, if you want everyone to know you're a junior varsity speaker, then start off with a joke. (We'll talk more about this later.)

 Great comedians always get a laugh in the first few seconds.

If you are a salesperson, then your opening line during initial contact is equally as important. As I stated earlier, never forget that getting a prospect to smile is like the door to do business opening to you.

Here are some interesting "pre-game" ideas I have collected that can help you build your "funny aura" before you ever go on stage.

★ Motivational humorist Brad Montgomery has a funny voicemail answering machine, and he has jokes at the bottom of his emails where people normally have their contact information. Salespeople can do this too.

★ Darren LaCroix sometimes sends humorous audio post-cards out to his audiences before he gets there.

★ Some speakers have video clips or PowerPoint slide shows of funny things up on screen before they come out on stage.

★ Many speakers have music playing to get the energy level of the crowd up.

Another huge part of creating a "funny aura" is to have some kind of a "shtick." David Glickman is a corporate comedian. He makes audiences laugh so hard that things come out their noses when he takes popular songs and re-writes the lyrics as customized jokes for an audience. On top of being brilliant and incredibly hard to do, his songwriting has also become David's shtick—it's what people remember him for. Popular comedians do the same thing: Jeff Foxworthy has "You might be a redneck," Larry the Cable Guy has "Git her done," and Bill Engvall has "Here's your sign."

Think about what your shtick could be that people would always remember you for. Mine is quickly becoming the mental exercise that I do with arranging the names of different popular items into a story.

Salespeople can develop funny auras also. My business partner and one of the co-founders of our motivational sales seminar company **Success Starts Now!**™, Gary Michels, has created some hilarious prospecting techniques that always get laughs. To many of the prospects who receive Gary's creative marketing mailers, he is known for this shtick.

Towards the end of this book I've included some of the best ones he came up with as well as a few others that I've encountered. You can find them in the section called *"The Funny 20."* It is 20 quick ways that salespeople can directly apply many of the concepts in this book to close more business.

Additionally, David Glickman's book *76 Ways to Keep Any Business Audience Laughing* is a phenomenal resource for things that will add to your funny aura. Glickman even includes some stock lines you can use for your introductions, and some very simple techniques to get that first quick laugh. I highly recommend it and use it frequently as a resource to help create an atmosphere that keeps people laughing because everyone else is laughing.

7. When They Are Shocked or Disgusted

Be careful with this one. Some comedians, speakers, and salespeople use this principle in a sleazy way to get laughs. Ed Tate, 2000 World Champion of Public Speaking once told me, "Rory, be cautious that you're never pimping your presentation just for a laugh." Realize that people will laugh when they are disgusted. However, they are laughing more so because the topic or language you're using makes them feel uncomfortable rather than because they think you're funny. They laugh as a release of tension.

You will often see beginning comedians rely on foul language or crude humor to help get a laugh. Obviously in a sales presentation or a business speech, you would never consider using foul language, but I have seen plenty of examples when a comedian inserted an obscenity into a joke that disgusted even a comedy club audience. Although there are a few expert comedians who use swear words effectively from time to time, this is incredibly rare and is something that we should probably avoid altogether. I encourage you to develop good material. Don't take the lazy way out by saying off-color or obscene phrases to get a laugh.

 "Be cautious that you're never pimping your presentation just for a laugh."

Now that we've covered that caveat, there are a few examples of shock that work and that illustrate this point well. The first one is from Robin Williams's HBO special, **Live at the Met**. Filmed in New York City, this routine was designed to be a little blue. During one of his bits, Robin took his bottled water and started shaking it so that water went flying out all over the stage. The joke is not important here, because my claim is simply that the shock of the water being sprayed everywhere added a brilliant touch to the delivery of the joke.

There are many examples where a comedian will use a mic or something else on stage as a prop that becomes another object. And people laugh because of the shock. In **Why You Crying?**, George Lopez uses the microphone cord at two different times, once as a nasal tube from an oxygen tank and another time in describing a male reproductive organ. Because of his skill at using shock, his bit is quite hysterical.

Similarly, I once heard of a salesperson who got laughs and made a sale by jumping up onto a chair to emphasize a point. While I don't recommend that you start going nuts in front of customers, the next time you are in someone's office, keep in the back of your mind the concept that the tactful use of shock and awe is a great way to make your audience laugh in the right situation.

8. Exaggerated Truth

One of the most common formulas you see in jokes is that somehow the punchline is an exaggeration of the truth. By taking something that could normally be reasonably true and stretching it, you can make things funny.

The first time I learned this was when I watched Roger Seip, President of Freedom Speakers and Trainers, doing the keynote speech at The Southwestern Company's sales school. He was telling a story about the first door he ever knocked on for a door-to-door sale. He said, "This gnarly face came to the door and peered out the window at me. This woman was probably seventy-five…thousand years old!"

Numbers often lend themselves to exaggerating the truth. I remember sitting around with some of my buddies after a night of partying, talking about my friend who had made a new lady friend the night before. He said, "Come on guys, she wasn't that bad. She was about a 6 or 7." Just then one of my other friends chimed in, "Yeah…out of 1000." Very funny.

A real estate agent named Sarah who attended my humor course recently said that she was convinced that she had once won a deal using this principle. Sarah said that her prospect had been really price sensitive, and as a result, they had been working together to find the right house for a long time. She recalled that she was showing her disheartened client a slightly overpriced house that fit all of his other requirements, and then she told the client that the home cost "$1.2 million...and 27 cents!" Sarah said that in that very moment she noticed a complete change in her customer's demeanor. By lightening the mood the customer finally decided to make the purchase. Using humor to really impact people is no joke.

Often when you are writing your speech or sales presentation you will automatically notice places that lend themselves to exaggerating the truth. Take advantage of these times. It is a very simple way to get a chuckle.

9. A Feeling of Superiority

Many late night talk show hosts get laughs by giving their audiences a feeling of superiority. That is, they cut down high ranking public officials, over-paid athletes, and senseless celebrities. These people, who are commonly seen as powerful or famous, suddenly become easy targets for humor, because bringing them down makes the rest of us feel superior.

This is why you hear so many jokes about the President, Michael Jackson, Catholic Priests, Mike Tyson, etc. In fact, one way to know that you are becoming famous is when comedians start making jokes about you.

One of my biggest laughs comes when I'm telling a true story about the time I was driving at 60 miles per hour and hit a cow that was standing in the middle of the road. When I explain that the officer arrived to the scene I say, "*He had this look* [perplexed facial expression]… like **Jessica Simpson on Jeopardy**." It gets a huge laugh every time. Jessica Simpson is gorgeous, rich, and famous, so everybody loves a cheap shot at a big dog. It just makes us feel better about being us.

Another brilliant example comes from Michael Kerr, a General Session speaker at the 2006 National Speakers Association (NSA) convention in Orlando, FL. There is an inside joke at NSA about all the silly designations, like MBA, CFP, CPA, and so on.

The highest ranking designation a professional speaker can earn is called a CSP, Certified Speaking Professional. Achieving this rank is an amazing honor that tells the world that you're a great speaker. As a result, there is sometimes an ego associated with the designation. Well, Michael is on stage and talking about CSPs. As he's describing what a CSP is, he takes out a balloon and starts to blow it up as a representation of someone's head as they're earning their CSP. By poking fun at CSPs, he makes all the non-CSPs feel better about themselves and gets a huge laugh. This may not be funny to you, but to a room full of speakers, it was hilarious. What was even more hysterical was how he topped himself by later using a callback (see next technique).

Even if you're selling to an individual, be sensitive to ways that you can poke fun at yourself or at a situation in order to help your prospect feel better about just being who they are.

10. Callbacks

Callbacks are one of the most enjoyable parts of writing comedy, and all of the great comedians use callbacks. A callback is when you find some way to tie in a previous joke that you used and got a laugh on into the punchline of another joke that you tell later. You are calling back the earlier reference. Callbacks have an amazing power, because the audience loves to make the connection. Callbacks also seem to create an illusion that what has just happened was for that audience and that audience only, and audiences love that as well.

To finish the story about the balloon incident at NSA, later on that same day Mike just so happened to be awarded with his CSP. When he walked out onto stage to receive his medal and plaque, the whole room was filled with astonishment and respect (tension) for the people on stage. Then, as they walked off the stage, Michael pulled out the same balloon from that morning and blew it up. The room exploded with laughter! It was one of the funniest moments I've ever been a part of. He was calling back to that original joke without saying a word. Absolutely brilliant.

If you watch closely you will notice that your friends and family use callbacks all the time in your everyday life. For example say you had used the "27 cents" line with one of your prospects when doing a price build-up as Sarah did. And say that it got a solid chuckle the first time. Then anytime you told that person the price of anything (such as additional fees associated with the purchase of a house) you could always pause and add "and 27 cents." It doesn't matter how many times you do this, you would almost always get a laugh. That is a callback. I promise you that using callbacks is an enjoyable way to interact with and sell to people.

In one of the speeches I gave to get to the World Championships of Public Speaking for Toastmasters I had a great callback. I told the story that is at the beginning of this book about my childhood and being raised by a single mother who sold Mary Kay. Later, when I'm talking about how I grew up to become a door-to-door salesperson I say, "I know that's bad, but I never wanted to go door-to-door. I was a perfectly normal child…I wanted to sell Mary Kay." Boom…just like that you light the audience up with a very special treat.

Callbacks are one of the great joys of comedy, whether on stage or in a selling situation, and they really make you feel like a professional.

 All of the great comedians use callbacks.

Chapter Three -
The 7 Lasting Laws
of Humor

Humor has a lot to do with a person's individual style and flavor. However, over the years I have noticed a collection of principles that always hold true in regards to getting laughs. The following concepts are not theories; they are laws. They are laws because they apply in every situation to every speaker, comedian, or salesperson. Some of these ideas are clichés in the professional speaking world because they are so often repeated. Meanwhile, a few are themes that I have intuitively noticed that apply to virtually every person trying to get a laugh.

Law #1: Humor Convergence

Now that you know why people laugh, the next logical question is: "Why do you laugh harder at some things than others?" I wondered this myself for a very long time before I finally figured it out; it's called humor convergence.

What causes big laughs are jokes that are able to combine many of the previously listed principles all into one concise bang. For example, let's look at my Jessica Simpson joke. If you put that joke up to our checklist of reasons why people laugh, you will understand this first law.

In the setup of the joke, I say, *"The officer just looked at me,"* and I give the audience a perplexed look. So I have created an expectation for the audience that I'm going to say something like "confused or shocked," which would've worked but wouldn't have been funny. The punchline of **"like Jessica Simpson on Jeopardy"** is a change in expectation; they didn't see it coming.

Also, note that the mind thinks through the process as follows: "Jessica Simpson = stupid; Jeopardy = smart show." This joke gives the audience mental exercise and the laugh comes when the audience "gets it." Next, Jessica Simpson and Jeopardy are two completely unrelated and never previously before associated terms. Finally, with the long pause on the facial expression I am creating tension. Anytime a speaker is silent on stage, artificial tension builds in the room. So I create the tension with the pause and then pop it with the punchline.

This joke gets an average laugh of 11 seconds from an audience if there are at least 400 people in the room. Why? Because of Why We Laugh Reason #6, you laugh because everyone else is laughing. As long as the room is setup properly, the joke works. This joke also meets Why We Laugh Reason #9, feeling of superiority. Combined, that means this joke capitalizes on six of the reasons why people laugh, and that's why it works; it's called humor convergence.

Law #2: Great jokes aren't written, they're re-written.

This is probably the oldest, most well-known, and most painfully accurate quote in the comedy kingdom. Every great joke or laugh line, whether it is in a comedy routine, a professional speech, or a sales presentation, has to be re-worked, re-invented, and re-tried several times before it reaches its potential.

When you watch Jerry Seinfeld on TV, his comedy looks very natural and un-rehearsed. In reality, he has tested the jokes that make it into his stand up routine hundreds if not thousands of times. Humor takes time, discipline, and practice.

Don't give up if you write a line and it doesn't work the first time you use it on a sales prospect, in a classroom, or to an audience. Keep at it. Chances are that if you think it's funny, then it probably is. You simply need to package the line in a way that will get an audience to laugh. Woody Allen said that for every 10 jokes he writes, one might be worth keeping and trying, and only one out of every 10 of those will actually make it on stage in a paid performance. Even the best have to struggle very hard at this, especially when they are trying something for the first time.

> Don't give up if you write a line and it doesn't work the first time you use it.

Law #3: The fewer words you use, the bigger the laugh.

Darren LaCroix says, "A laugh is inversely proportionate to the number of words it takes to get there." He is so right. When you write a setup and a punchline, you need to cut every unnecessary word. You need to find a way to rearrange the phrase so that it takes as few words as possible to get to the punch. Every single word matters.

I originally wrote one of my jokes like this:

"When I was just a little boy my mom bought a set of books for me called the Volume Library. The Volume Library was kind of like encyclopedias except it helped with the 'how to' more than the who, what, when, and where. I used to love those books and I used them all the time. I used them to learn about math. I loved to flip through the science section for all the experiments, ***and I liked to look at all the pictures of the naked people from Africa***."

In that version it takes me 90 words to get through the punchline. And while the joke is funny, the punchline is watered down because it takes forever to get there. Five months later, after being mentored by some of the worlds greatest speech writers like David Brooks, here is what I came up with:

*"The Volume Library was a set of encyclopedia-type reference books that my mom bought me as a kid. I loved it growing up, because it had math, and science, and **naked people.**"*

This version has only 32 words. It is tight, it is punchy, it is professional, and it is funny. The fewer the words you use, the bigger the laugh you'll get.

Rearrange the phrase so that it takes as few words as possible to get to the punch.

Law #4: The more specific the humor, the more terrific the humor.

This law is a direct quote from David Glickman, and it captures the essence of what his company does. Audiences like knowing that your presentation has been written just for them and is not canned. However, this is in conflict with some of the other laws, because it's near impossible to create new jokes for every speech.

However, in exchange for a spontaneous or customized joke, an audience is forgiving and is willing to laugh harder, even if the punchline is not as good. There are a few brilliant and highly skilled people who I have seen that are able to create this customized humor every time. David Glickman and Brad Montgomery are two I have already mentioned. Another, who is one of the best in the world at this and possibly the funniest man on the planet, is NSA's bad boy Dale Irvin.

These three guys are incredible. They interview people at your office, school, or organization and find out your pain points and frustrations, and then they create a whole bunch of jokes just for your group. While they make a career out of it, you and I can just take a small piece of it.

Whether you are going to do a sales presentation for a big client or be a guest speaker for an organization, do some research ahead of time and find out some of the current events that have been happening with your audience. For example, maybe someone just got married, had a baby, or got a promotion. These are great opportunities to create something specific just for that group—something only they would understand and get.

One example of this was when I spoke at a conference where

the theme was ALOHAS! I got to the site a few hours early like I always do. My jaw dropped to the floor when I saw how affectionate and close knit this group was. They were laughing and hugging and singing and just kind of all warm and fuzzy. So when I walked out on stage I said, "I just found out that your theme ALOHAS is actually an acronym. It stands for Always Lots Of Hugging And Singing." It's not funny here in print, but the audience blew the roof off with laughter.

I could've said anything for the next hour. It didn't matter because they loved me already. They thought everything I said was funny, and we had a great time because I took two minutes to really go out of my way to connect with them. That is the power, the challenge, and the enjoyment you can get from humor. Remember, the audience or your sales prospect will love it, even if the joke is not as good, because you're making them feel special.

 In exchange for a spontaneous or customized joke, an audience is forgiving.

Law #5: Stage Time

Darren LaCroix likes to say, "Stage time, stage time, stage time." When I first got started in this business Eric Chester said to me, "Really the only thing that matters is stage time. The difference between a good speaker and a great speaker is 1,000 speeches." It seemed like that was the only thing he said to me the first ten times we talked. So I guess it *is* all about stage time.

Stage time can literally mean being on a stage or it can mean telling a story at a dinner table to a group of friends. The point is to never miss out on your opportunity to share a story with others. Why is this so important? Because you can try out jokes. Even better, your friends will often insert comments that you can re-work into great jokes.

Getting on stage is how you get comfortable, and the more you do it, the more comfortable you get. You may not believe this just yet, but you really are a funny person. In fact, you're hilarious. You do dumb stuff all the time that makes you laugh like crazy. You have some of the silliest thoughts that just warm your soul. Now you're simply learning how to be so comfortable that you can be your goofy self in front of an audience of 1 or 1,000. Eddie Brill, talent coordinator for The Late Show with David Letterman, taught me that the one difference that separates the greats from everyone else is vulnerability. The person who is comfortable enough to just be their uninhibited self in front of a group is the one the audience is going to fall in love with. People appreciate vulnerability and what it takes to get there is stage time.

When you're trying to write humor, don't sit and think it up; rather, capture the humor that happens to you in everyday life. The more stage time you have, the more humor you will accidentally stumble upon, and the better you will get at delivering your deliberately intended jokes. Without stage time the rest of the principles in this book are worthless. It's all about stage time. Period.

 The person who is comfortable enough to just be their uninhibited self in front of a group is the one the audience is going to fall in love with.

Law #6: Jokes do not make you funny; don't waste time stealing them.

Most people think being funny means telling jokes. Nothing could be further from the truth. Anyone can tell a joke; but it takes a lot of focus and creativity to be funny. The problem with jokes is that half of the audience has already heard it. Twenty-five percent of the audience will hear it and not get it, not care, or just be offended. The rest of the group will get it, but some of them some of them won't think it's funny.

The worst part about jokes, though, is that they're usually stolen. Like I said, it's a skill to be able to develop something funny, and that's what we're after. Now don't get me wrong…I enjoy jokes. I like telling them in casual conversation with my friends. But this is business, and we have to be a little more advanced than that. We need to challenge ourselves to come up with things that are funny; and that's what you're learning now.

Also, please NEVER steal someone else's funny material. Feel free to steal old jokes if you wish, and you can freely share certain stock lines that every one uses. But the fastest way to lose respect from speakers or professionals who would probably help you out is to steal their funny material. In the long run, it's always better for you, more fun, and simple enough to write your own stuff.

One final note: You'll notice that many of the principles, concepts, and examples I use in this book are from other places, but I always give credit to the source. You can use a funny quote and maybe occasionally someone else's joke if you give credit, but taking other people's stuff doesn't make you a funny person; it makes you a thief.

Law #7: Capturing humor is easier than writing it.

The 1990 World Champion of Public Speaking, David Brooks, says that if you're not a funny person then "find what makes you laugh, and then find a way to share it with others."

Chances are that more than once in your life you have had a thought that you knew was hilarious; you just knew it. Or maybe something happened to you in real life that was funnier than anything you could ever make up. Often when I'm doing presentations something happens with the audience or I say something funny, and everyone laughs accidentally. If you can figure out a way to capture these moments when they happen, then it will not take long before you have a deep file of funny material.

The easiest way to capture humor is to write it down. Every good comedian carries a notebook and writes down all the random funny thoughts that occur throughout the day. Have you ever watched a comedian tell a joke and thought to yourself, "Yes, that is so true!"? That joke probably came from a real life situation that happened to the comedian, who was disciplined enough to write it down.

Think of how much fun you would have as a salesperson if you were writing down all of the funny things or people you encountered as part of your job. Anything that makes you laugh spontaneously can be re-worked and used again later. So, as you write these things down, don't worry about forming it into a punchline when it happens; just capture what made you laugh. If you don't write it down right then, I guarantee that you will forget it. So capture it in the moment and arrange it into a punchline later.

Another characteristic of all of the best speakers in the world is that they video record their presentation whenever they can. Sometimes they do it simply for evaluation purposes or for promotional footage, but another great reason to videotape yourself is that spontaneous things will happen when you're presenting that are hysterical. And if you can watch those moments as they occur, you can often find a way to re-create them on purpose in later presentations. This is essentially what happened with my sales presentations when I was going door-to-door. After 5 years and 15,000 demonstrations, my sales presentation was basically a compilation of funny lines I was using that came from, what was at one time, spontaneous situations.

If you give the same sales presentation or stage presentation over and over, the same is guaranteed to be true for you. If you are able to capture these accidental occurrences, then eventually you will have a final product that sparkles.

 So capture it in the moment and arrange it into a punchline later.

Chapter Four -
Overcoming the
Fear of Humor

A few people in the world are not afraid to try anything during a presentation; however, the majority of people will only try humor if they are almost positive it will work. Why? As Brad Montgomery explains, "Because humor feels so risky. It's a horrible feeling to say something that is supposed to be funny, and everyone knows it was supposed to be funny, yet nobody's laughing. That's called bombing."

Brad does customized corporate comedy, and although he is one of those people who is just naturally hilarious (and he is ab-workout hilarious) I've learned a tremendous amount about the appropriate attitude to take when trying humor. He teaches two key concepts that will help you overcome your fear of using humor.

Fear Fighter #1: Radar Principle

The first is what I refer to as the radar principle. This is analogous to a plane flying underneath the radar. Many people who are trying out a joke for the first time have so much anticipation about the joke that when they deliver it and it doesn't get a laugh, they freeze.

The freeze is the signal that it was supposed to be a joke. That moment is when everyone feels an incredibly awkward tension in the room. Well, if you deliver a joke and you pause for only half a second to see if it's going to get a laugh, then you can often avoid that awkwardness by just rolling right along. The philosophy here is that if no one laughed they obviously didn't think it was a joke (or a good one anyway), so don't signal to them that it was.

Fear Fighter #2: The Frasier Rule

From 1993-2004, NBC ran a sitcom called *Frasier*. This was one of Brad Montgomery's all-time favorite shows. But here's the interesting part about it: Brad never laughed out loud when he watched that show. Even though he watched it religiously, and he enjoyed it thoroughly, he hardly ever laughed.

This takes us back to the opening discussion of this book about the challenge of measuring funny. It's very difficult to measure funny, and you can only measure laughs. However, just because someone isn't laughing out loud doesn't necessarily mean they didn't think you were funny. If you remember, the technical advantage of laughter is simply to restore the audience's attention and focus. By being willing to try jokes you may be effectively accomplishing that even though you might not be getting a laugh.

Haven't you ever heard someone say something where you didn't laugh out loud but inside you thought to yourself, "Ha! That was funny." There is a good chance that people who are in your audience are doing the same thing; *especially* if you are in a one-on-one situation with a prospect.

Realize that it's much harder to make one person laugh out loud than it is to make 1,000 people laugh out loud. Remember that people often laugh because everyone else is laughing. You don't have that luxury in a one-on-one situation.

To me, the Frasier rule is incredibly powerful, because it helps us realize that even though we may not be getting a laugh, there is still a fairly good chance that people see us as being funny.

Fear Fighter #3: Aren't you an audience member?

Another incredibly empowering paradigm shift came to me from 1990 World Champion of Public Speaking David Brooks. David asks all of his students a very simple question, "Do you think the audience is for or against you?"

I have to admit that when I first started speaking, I honestly thought the audience wanted me to fail. Okay, maybe they didn't want to fail, but they wanted to challenge me, as in, "Alright, let's see what this guy's got."

David changed my whole perspective with five words. "Aren't you an audience member?" When we watch a performance or a movie, or even meet someone one-on-one for the first time, we don't tell ourselves, "I hope this person is lame." Unless you as the salesperson or speaker have given the audience some reason to think that you're arrogant, they will most likely be thinking, "Oh, I hope this guy is really good," or "I hope this gal is really funny."

Having this understanding of the audience's frame of mind changes everything for you as a presenter. This attitude makes you feel like the audience is on your side, like they want you to succeed, and it helps you to talk to them instead of at them.

Fear Fighter #4: Welcome to the club.

Now that you have an understanding of a few reasons why you should be comfortable with the fear of using humor let me burst your bubble. There are going to be times when you try something and it is simply not funny. It seemed funny to you when you were planning it out but when you deliver it, everyone knows it was supposed to be funny and it's not. Welcome to the club.

Every single person who has ever tried humor has at one point said something that was intended to be funny that didn't end up turning out the way they hoped. Everyone. One of the best lessons I ever received was by watching a documentary about Jerry Seinfeld called "Comedian."

"Comedian" is not a funny movie. In fact, there are times when it is painful because it shows the behind the scenes process of what it takes to be a comedian. In the movie you see live clips of Jerry Seinfeld trying to get 5 minutes at an open mic night and then getting on stage and just bombing! This happens to everyone. You cannot be funny until you've mastered being unfunny; some of us get there faster than others.

 There are going to be times when you try something and it is simply not funny.

Fear Fighter #5 - Saver Lines

The previous four Fear Fighter shifts are all focused on making you feel okay about not getting laughs. This one, once learned properly, will make you excited about not getting laughs. That's right, excited.

We have already mentioned that when you tell a joke and it doesn't go over, the room is instantly filled with an incredibly awkward tension. Everyone knows what you just said was supposed to be a joke, but nobody laughed, except maybe the drunk guy in the corner. Mark the following words of brilliance. "By telling a joke that wasn't funny, you have just created an opportunity to be hilarious!"

Why? Because you have artificially created tension in the room. What do we know about tension? People laugh as an exhale of tension. When you tell a joke that bombs, it is like the room is taking a deep inward breath. Then, when you immediately acknowledge the cause of that tension (your recently crappy joke), you pop that bubble and the room exhales in the form of a huge laugh. This is called a saver line.

The most well known master of saver lines is Johnny Carson. Many of my comedy mentors have used him as an example, because when he would tell a joke that was bad, he would just wait and smile, and then completely win you back with his saver line.

We talked earlier about how you never steal jokes from comedians or humorists. The one caveat to that is with saver lines. Saver lines are largely considered in the industry to be stock, public domain lines, for everyone to use. You don't have to use stock lines, though. You can come up with your own. But you are welcome to use other people's if you want.

Some of my favorite saver lines are:

- ★ *Some of these jokes I tell are just for me.*
- ★ *Boy, I was looking for a nice quiet place to practice.* – David Glickman
- ★ *I thought that'd be funnier.* – Darren LaCroix
- ★ *Oooh. Cross that one off the funny list.* – Brad Schlepp
- ★ *Or not.* – Brad Montgomery
- ★ *That was subliminal humor. You're not laughing, but you're liminals are cracking up!* – Brad Montgomery
- ★ *Alright.* – Mitch Hedberg
- ★ *That joke is going to be funny because I'm going to take all the words out, and add new words.* – Mitch Hedberg
- ★ *That's okay, I can wait.* – David Glickman
- ★ *Is this thing on? (tap the mic)* – David Glickman

You can use saver lines in more situations than when you tell a bad joke; you can use one anytime you notice tension. Simply acknowledge what created the tension. Some tension building examples are: a bad joke, a fire alarm, a cell phone, a baby crying, a heckler, and many more. In fact, a great exercise is to keep a running list of situations that happen to you when you're presenting, and then think of something to say that's funny later so that next time it happens you are ready. This concept is called planned spontaneity.

Saver lines also work quite well in small groups or one-on-one situations. I'm amazed at how many times I've told a funny story at a dinner table that ended up not being funny, and I end up getting a laugh on the saver line. To me, it doesn't really matter where people laugh, as long as they laugh. Most of the time they're not going to remember what they laughed at, just that they were laughing.

There is one important key to how you deliver a saver line: you have to pause. This is contradictory to the *radar principle*, where you roll through it. Once you are experimenting and learning how to use saver lines, you definitely want to freeze. Why? Because a saver line will only work if there is tension in the room. If you deliver your bad joke and then your saver line immediately following it, you will have a *double dump*.

So deliver the joke, and then once it fails, sit tight. This takes an extraordinary amount of discipline at first, because you have to just sit and be with that incredible uncomfortable ness for half a second longer than you want to, and then bang! You deliver the saver line. Saver lines are all about mastering that timing.

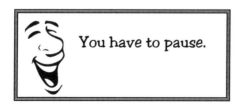
You have to pause.

Chapter Five -
The Magic
Humor Toolbox

We have spent a good deal of time so far on the concept of "why people laugh." After all, it's useless to simply have a book of jokes. If you are just stealing jokes then you have no real skill, because you are always at the whim of other people for your material. The power in this book is that you are learning how to create your own material, which is much more valuable to your future success.

The next step is to go from the theory and the concepts of why people laugh into the practical application. The golden gift I'm going to give to you here is some universal formulas for humor that I have ciphered from my in depth study of laughter. For even more humor coaching, please visit **www.ssnseminars.com** (shameless plug).

The formulas presented here are universal, and they are guaranteed to work. All you have to do is insert new objects or ideas into them and you will get laughs tomorrow. Once again, this is not easy, yet with this toolbox it becomes incredibly simple. The best way to use this toolbox is to take any of your finished speeches or sales presentations written out and run it against this checklist. You will naturally find that some parts of your presentations will lend themselves to these formulas.

Formula #1: Funny Words and Numbers

Going along our school of thought that adding humor doesn't always mean getting out loud laughter is the technique of funny words. Realize that some words are just funnier than others. You have so many opportunities to exchange a boring word with a funny one. You simply need to recognize these moments. When you do, you'll add some color and dimension to your talk and possibly get a laugh.

For example, "Winnebago" is a funny word, as is "chimpanzee." Dane Cook makes a living off of funny words in his routine; he is a master at taking what would usually be a boring sentence and making it into a hilarious string of uncommon words that are funny. To Dane, it's not an ice cream cone it's a "twisty cone." And we weren't getting into trouble; rather, we were "partaking in our normal shenanigans."

What makes a funny word? I don't really know; my best guess is that whatever you think is funny or uncommon (a change in expectation) from the terms people use every day counts as a funny word.

With that said, here are some general guidelines you can follow. First, words that have a hard "k" sound in them are often very funny, such as "monkey" or "macaroni." Words that have two of the same letter in a row tend to be funny, like "weezer" or "piddle." And "onomatopoeia" is always funny.

Onomatopoeia is when the word makes the same sound as the action that produces that sound. These are all those words you used to see on the old Batman and Robin TV show: "whack," "smack," "crack," "slap," "thud," etc. Whenever you are telling a story you can usually add one of these words very easily to lighten the mood.

Also, brand names are always funnier than generic. So, "I was sitting at home eating cereal and watching TV," becomes "It was one of those days where I was lounging in my La-Z-Boy eating Lucky Charms and watching Matlock." The latter is much funnier.

Odd numbers are also funnier than even numbers. No one knows why, but for some reason 11 is funnier than 10. Also rare numbers are funnier than common numbers. So instead of saying, "He's worth a million dollars," say, "He's worth like a million and 27 dollars."

You can always find some way to add funny words or numbers to your talk. One place you use numbers a lot as a salesperson is when you're talking about price. If you were selling a house that you're client really wanted and you knew it was a bit above their price range, you could say something like, "This house is one million two hundred thousand dollars….and 27 cents."

The regular delivery of your voice as you state the price creates an expectation, because the prospect assumes that the "one million two hundred thousand dollars" is all (s)he is going to hear. Then you change the expectation by adding on "and 27 cents" at the end. This would work particularly well if upon relaying the price, your prospect seemed to slump or became discouraged, because that would create additional tension that could be released.

Realize that you likely won't make people fall out of their chairs laughing, but surely the addition of "27 cents" would get a chuckle. And sometimes as a salesperson or a speaker, a chuckle is all you need. A simple smile can make all the difference in closing a multi-million dollar account or in causing a contagious spread of laughter in a large audience.

Formula #2: Acronyms

Hallelujah and praise the humor gods when you find an acronym. Acronyms are the easiest and some of the funniest laughs you will ever get. Seriously, if you are speaking to a group or a person that uses acronyms (I've yet to find one that doesn't) then you have an absolute freebie. You are really blowing an opportunity for humor if you don't capitalize on acronyms.

The technique is very simple. Take the acronym as it regularly stands and just give it entirely new words that begin with the same letter. An acronym automatically functions as a setup, because everyone who knows the acronym has the pre-set expectation of what it means. By changing the acronym you will not only be funny, but if you can tailor it, you also look like a genius. The audience will not only love it, but they will also remember you for it.

For example, if you are talking to an audience that travels a lot, then you can say something about the security at airports. Bring up TSA, the security people, and say something like, "When I was being herded through airport security the other day I finally figured something out. Do you know what TSA really stands for? **T**housands **S**tanding **A**round." While that might not be hilarious to you, many audiences will absolutely love it.

Another one of my best jokes is about getting my M.B.A. I say, "I recently got my MBA (pause for inauthentic clapping), and I figured out that MBA really stands for **M** **B**roke **A**gain." I get a laugh on that every time.

The key here is to expose some sort of pain point, frustration, or obviousness that exists. Since airport security is such a hassle for everyone, I am introducing the common frustration (tension) of TSA, and popping it with the new definition. With MBA, I'm creating the tension or expectation of my ego, and then popping it with self deprecating humor that, even though I'm supposed to be successful, I'm really broke like everyone else.

You can play with acronyms all day. It is a fun exercise and a great way to get laughs. Without a doubt, your workplace or your profession probably has a ton of these quirky little acronyms you can use. Think of the acronyms you use on a daily basis and challenge yourself to re-write them somehow.

 Acronyms are the easiest and some of the funniest laughs you will ever get.

Formula #3: The Rule of 3

If there were any ancient literary works or stone tablets about humor you would find that the rule of three is the oldest, most common, and still one of the most effective tools to get a laugh. Every comedian or funny person I've ever watched uses the rule of three, even if they don't know they do it. The rule of three applies to anytime you are listing examples.

The first two items in the sequence function as the setup for the joke and are two items that the audience would normally expect to hear in that list. Then, the third item functions as the punchline and is somehow twisted from the first two. That is where you get the laugh.

Earlier, we dissected an opening line from one of my World Championship Speeches that used the rule of three. The line was, "I loved the Volume Library because it had math, and science, and naked people." Math and science are two topics that are normally referred to as school subjects. The third item, naked people, is a twist to that because it is true, but unexpected, and not commonly associated with math or science. Typically, you would expect to hear something like history or reading to complete the list.

Notice, though, that "naked people" is only a stretch of the truth. It is ketchup when the audience is expecting a tomato. If the third item had been "Jumanji," then it wouldn't work as well. Although "Jumanji" is a funny word and popular movie title, it is too far removed from math and science. That is more like olive juice instead of ketchup. Naked people, however, does the same thing for virtually everyone; it takes their minds directly to the old National Geographic magazines that almost every kid looked at to see naked people from around the globe.

One of my all time favorite examples of a rule of three is from Darren LaCroix when he tells the story of how he switched from being a comedian to a speaker. He says, "These new audiences (specifically Toastmasters) were nice, they were encouraging, and they were sober." Anyone who knows Toastmasters really gets this, because it is an organization that is commonly known to display overwhelming happiness and enthusiastic encouragement. And if you've ever been to a comedy club, then you get the joke.

So the rule of three is one way that paints the façade of spontaneity, when in fact the joke is meticulously written and rehearsed. If you wrote out your sales talk or your stage presentation right now, I'm sure you would find at least one place where you are using a list of some sort. Find a way to shorten that list to three, and then insert a twisted third item at the end to create a punchline.

Formula #4: Visual Images

The human mind thinks in pictures. When someone says, "ice cream cone," your mind probably visualizes a cone with a scoop of ice cream on top.   You don't see the letters "i-c-e c-r-e-a-m c-o-n-e" flash through your mind. Knowing that the mind thinks in pictures allows you to realize that one of your greatest tools in getting laughs is to purposefully create funny pictures in your audience's minds.

The great thing about this technique is that you can either use funny images from your real life that have actually happened, or you can create imaginary ones out of thin air. Remember my "Amish family pulling up in a Hummer" line? While that is funny because they are two disassociated topics, it is also funny (humor convergence) because it creates a funny picture of an Amish family in their homemade clothes driving this huge beast of a machine.

Similes often lend themselves to create funny visual images. "She was as dumb as a sack of hammers." "I was drenched like a soggy Cocoa Puff." "I'd rather hop across the north pole on a pogo stick." These are all somewhat silly, but effective (in the right circumstances), as funny visual images.

Leveraging this tool can be the difference between why you always end your stories with "I guess you had to be there" when your funny friend has the crowd in stitches. I've noticed that in public conversation, the people who are funny without knowing why have a way of naturally painting a vivid picture of a funny situation. Now that you know this, you can deliberately do the same thing.

Creating visual images is another tool that not only helps you to get more laughs, but it also helps you to be a better presenter. If you are selling something, then you know that most people buy on emotion and not on logic. If you are able to paint clear pictures then you touch on the emotion and have dramatically enhanced your chance to make a sale. If you are speaking to an

> Creating visual images is another tool that not only helps you to get more laughs, but it also helps you to be a better presenter.

audience, then images increase your chances of keeping your listeners awake.

Formula #5: Facial Expressions

If the rule of three is the single most common humor formula, then facial expression is the single most under utilized technique by people trying to get laughs. Adding a facial expression to any story or point is huge! You can get some of your biggest laughs by learning to over exaggerate your facial expressions.

Obviously, it is hard to give great examples of facial expressions in writing, but watch Bill Cosby or Jim Carrey and you will see the mastery of the facial expression. Going overboard with a facial expression is another thing that is naturally outside the realm of expectation in normal everyday conversation. So all you need to do is capture one of those silly faces you've been making your whole life and bring it into different parts of your presentation.

If you're in sales you could say something like, "Doing business with me is the difference between going home to your spouse and getting a smile versus getting one of these [arms crossed over exaggerated look of disapproval]." When I'm on stage one of my biggest laughs comes when I'm telling a story about a car accident I was in. All I say is, "If you've never been in an accident, there's a special moment right before impact, that looks a lot like this [oh, s#!* face]!" You would be amazed at how much that adds to a presentation and how simple it is to do.

Again, simple doesn't mean easy, and the reason why people never use this formula is because a facial expression is risky. If it's over exaggerated and doesn't get a laugh, then that creates some incredible tension, and that's why people shy away from it. What's different about you now, though, is that you understand that if you've just created tension by not being funny, then you have an opportunity to be hilarious with a saver line. Maybe something like, "Sorry, that's the face my spouse gave me this morning and it's stuck in my head." Whatever it is, the saver line wouldn't have to be that good because the tension would be so high.

Start watching the facial expressions of people in your everyday life. Notice how animated some of them are and challenge yourself to take note of the goofy expressions you make throughout the day. If nothing else, you'll have a riot laughing at yourself.

Formula #6: Fast Lists

Another incredibly simple and commonly used technique for getting laughs is to write fast lists. Your list doesn't even have to be something funny, but the fact that you put a bunch of items together in a series and are able to recite it quickly and without thinking makes people laugh. Most likely this is because of the mental exercise concept introduced earlier, in which audience members have to think fast to keep up with what you are saying.

My most famous joke is a fast list. When I talk about being raised by a single mother who sold Mary Kay I say, "Ladies every morning, (fast) wash, toner, moisturizer, foundation, wrinkle free eye cream, base eye shadow, dark eye shadow, blush, eyeliner, mascara, lip liner, and lipstick." For some reason people love this joke. And what's amazing is that they will remember me years later when they see me as "the guy who did the makeup thing."

While I'm sad to say that my 15 minutes of fame comes from knowing more about makeup than I know about any other manly item, it does accomplish the purpose of getting a laugh and helping people to remember me.

A great friend of mine and one of my early students, Nancy Spurry, weaved together a brilliant fast list of all the acronyms of the different software certifications she has and the different terms she uses as an employee of IBM. Her application of this technique gets a laugh every single time.

One way to emphasize the laugh with this technique is to make the last item in a fast series some sort of a twist from all the others. If you have parallel construction or some common theme throughout the whole list then you can easily find an item that is a slight switch.

1999 World Champion of Public Speaking Craig Valentine does exactly that with this fast sequence when he's talking about the power of writing down your goals: "I said I wanted to be a full time professional speaker; I'm a full time professional speaker. I said I wanted to own my own business; I own my own business. I said I wanted a beautiful wife; I have a beautiful wife. I said I wanted a white Mercedes-Benz convertible; *I have a white Honda Accord*. I'm getting there."

A practical application of this as a salesperson might be when you are reading the stipulations of a contract. You could memorize a bunch of jargon and recite it really quickly, maybe throwing

 Make the last item in a fast series some sort of a twist from all the others.

a funny word in the middle that doesn't fit or having some sort of twist at the end. There are many places in your presentations, sales talks, and even everyday conversations where you use lists, so think of how you can take advantage of this technique.

Formula #7: Self-Deprecating

Tying into the concept of creating a feeling of superiority, a great way to get laughs is always at your own expense. Self-deprecating humor is really the only type of humor that is almost always safe. The only time it is not safe is when it becomes the whole focus of your talk, because then it becomes distracting and people don't know whether to laugh or feel sorry for you.

Ninety-five percent of the time, though, you are going to win points by making light of yourself. There is an unspoken yet understood rule in comedy that if you make fun of yourself first, you have a license to make fun of whatever or whomever you want after.

This is slightly less tangible than the other formulas because there are so many ways to be self-deprecating. The best way to come up with this material is to ask yourself, "What would somebody make fun of me for?" Just like making a sale, you want to answer the objection before it comes up, and by making fun of yourself for all of the ways that you fit into a stereotype you eliminate the audience's opportunity to make fun of you in a mean way. You actually forward the process of getting them to laugh with you, eliminating their chance to laugh at you.

I make the argument that being self-deprecating actually raises your credibility with an audience, because it shows that you don't take yourself too seriously. It also shows that you are in tune with reality, even as it applies to yourself.

One of my favorite ways to use self-deprecating humor is to let the audience know of one of my accomplishments, and then to burst the ego bubble that I have created. For example I say things like, "At age 12 I became the youngest black belt in Colorado to ever get beaten up by a girl." "I became a door-to-door salesperson. We're like the human version of email spam."

This gives me credibility by letting people know about my accomplishments and creates a great opportunity for humor. One of the other really important keys is to bring up what other people are thinking.

Ronald Reagan once leveraged this principle in such a way that many people say it actually won him an election. He was behind in the voting to a much younger candidate and had been under intense pressure because of his age. Brilliantly, during one of the nationally televised debates he led off with a statement that went something like this, "I realize that there has been some discussion about the age of the candidates in this race, and I want to officially announce that I do not plan to expose the youth and inexperience of my opponent."

It killed. Not only did it get huge laughs (because the tension was so high), but it also answered an objection right up front in a way that showed power and presence. If a laugh can help you

 Self-deprecating humor actually raises your credibility with an audience, because it shows that you don't take yourself too seriously.

win a presidential election then it can certainly help close you a sale or win over an audience. That is what humor can do for you if used correctly in the appropriate situation.

Forumla#8: Finishers and Opposite Lines

Another easy way to add humor to almost any presentation is to look for places where you already have questions in your talk and add either a finisher line or an opposite line. With a finisher line, you ask a question, and then add on to the question. By doing this you are leveraging the concept of creating an expectation. The add-on is what changes it.

I've seen a few speakers use the following finisher line, and it works every time: "How many of you are married….and miserable?" The key to using this technique (as in delivering most jokes) is in the pause. You pause after what could be a question by itself, allow people's minds to begin to process what you've just asked, and then add a phrase on the end that switches the question's meaning. I've used lines like, "How many of you have had a salesperson at your door…that you tried to kill?"

If you're in front of a large group, make sure that you raise your hand as you're asking the question. This helps you to create momentum for people to raise their hands so they get caught in this embarrassment trap. By the way, embarrassment is a source of tension, and that is what causes the laugh here.

Another crucial part of the delivery with this technique is your voice. Your vocal intonation needs to be part of the setup for the joke. That means that you have to say the first part of the question in a way that sounds like you are really asking just that first part, because that creates the expectation. Then, your pause comes across to make it look like you were just finishing that thought and you added the twist.

Sometimes a chuckle is all you need.

Now let's move on to opposite lines. 1999 World Champion of Public Speaking Craig Valentine taught me one of the simplest ways to add good humor that's appropriate for almost any situation. It's called an opposite line. Many times when you ask someone a question, and then ask them the opposite of that question, it is very funny.

For example, in a sales presentation you might naturally ask someone, "Would it be nice if you could save some money on this?" After a long pause you could follow it up with something like, "Or would you prefer to have all your cash completely wiped out?" The obviousness and silliness of the answer to the second question juxtaposed with the seriousness of the answer to the first question creates the laugh.

Once again, depending on how good your questions are this may or may not get a huge laugh, but it can certainly bring a chuckle. And like I mentioned before, sometimes a chuckle is all you need.

Formula #9: Current Affairs

I mentioned earlier that when you're using a saver line the audience is much more forgiving. That is, they'll give you a bigger laugh even if your joke is not brilliant, because they are rewarding the spontaneity, whether it is authentic or planned. Another time an audience follows this same rule is when you sneak in something about a current affair.

This is precisely what the night time television show hosts do. Every night they do a news broadcast for you, except they make a joke out of every story. They get laughs because they are incorporating current affairs. The audience knows that, like saver lines or planned spontaneity, the joke is good for a limited time only.

Sometimes you will accidentally find ways to work in current affairs. For example, I was delivering a speech at a university the day after Vice President Cheney shot his friend during their hunting expedition. In my speech I had never planned on getting a laugh, but I had a line that I had said thousands of times in my speech that went like this: "Life's all about developing skills, and some people just don't have any skills."

Without thinking I said, "Vice President Cheney didn't get any hunting skills." To my surprise, the room exploded with laughter. As a stand alone punchline this was not anything even remotely brilliant, but in that situation it was a huge hit. This is similar to the principle we discussed earlier: "The more specific the humor, the more terrific the humor."

Professional summarizers like David Glickman and Dale Irvin often make genius use of these pop culture current affair gifts. You can do the same thing, and you will get great laughs by bringing something current up because you are conjoining unrelated ideas. You are relating whatever it is you are talking about to some current affair. Just keep your antenna up for these and every once in a while you'll stumble on to something great.

Formula #10: Gestures

Add gestures! Whether you are on stage addressing an audience or just talking to friends in everyday life, use gestures. Gestures add to the value of what you're saying by giving dimension to your words. Similar to facial expressions, gestures will get you laughs when you over exaggerate what the actual activity would really look like.

While almost all great comedians use gestures I am going to go back again to Jerry Seinfeld and Ellen DeGeneres. These two are the masters of gestures. Watch one of their stand-ups and just look how they add a gesture to almost every single joke they tell. Many times a gesture simply enhances a punchline, but sometimes the biggest laughs come when the gesture *is* the punchline.

Chapter Six -
The Humor
Exercises

Humor, just like any other skill, is a lot like a muscle; you can develop and strengthen it. You build muscles by breaking them down through struggle or exercises. There are a variety of ways to build your humor muscle, and here are some of the best.

Funny Lists

Humor, just like any other skill, is a lot like a muscle.

One thing you should absolutely do today is put up lists in your office. One list should be titled "funny words," another should be "funny references," and one should be your "acronym list." Having these lists displayed serves multiple purposes. First, they give you a place of reference to go to when you need to come up with a joke. Second, they turn on your reticular activating system so that you will start becoming more acutely aware of funny situations or thoughts that you have. Maybe the best reason for keeping these lists is because they will make you smile many times throughout the work day.

One saleswoman who was in my classes said that she has been keeping a list of "funny names" of actual people she has called on, and it is hilarious. Can you imagine? Anyone who has ever been in sales, especially cold calling, can have a deep appreciation for the wild names you run into. She kept it for no reason other than to make her smile. Now, she has a wealth of material to use when telling the stories, or when just speaking in casual situations.

Another great list to keep is a "situation list." Whenever you are in a presentation and some sort of event happens that throws you for a curve, that's another item for your situation list. These events often create tension, which is an opportunity for planned spontaneity. Darren LaCroix says, "If you can't think of something funny to say in the situation, just write the event down and you will think of something funny later." So at least the next time you'll be ready.

As mentioned earlier, you also might start a self-deprecating list of all your own little quirky characteristics. Have your friends, family, and co-workers help you with this for a fun activity in and of itself.

Evaluation

I can't stress to you enough how important it is to write out and record your presentation. Whether it is a speech or a sales presentation, write it out word for word. Just because you write it out word for word doesn't mean you have to present it word for word. This exercise simply forces you to communicate your thoughts in a concise way using powerful language. It also is a great way to develop humor accidentally!

Then, record yourself as often as possible. We have talked about how you will capture spontaneous moments of humor that you can re-create, but in evaluating yourself as you re-watch the film you will think, "Oh, I should've said that." Plus, I'm sure your sales manager or your speaking coach thinks that a little self-evaluation couldn't hurt.

Funny Games

One of the best humor exercises is to go out and buy a dictionary of clichés and re-write the endings. Any cliché functions as a great setup, because almost everyone already knows the cliché and/or has a strong expectation of how the phrase goes. By re-writing the end of clichés you are automatically creating jokes. You'll find that sometimes it's harder to find the setup than to let your funny little mind come up with a punchline. A dictionary of clichés takes care of this for you.

The "late night" game is something I developed to start thinking like a humorist. All you do is try to predict what jokes you are going to see on the late night talk shows. Even if you can't predict the jokes, see if you can at least predict the topics that the late night hosts are going to hit on. This is another way of programming yourself to think funny.

 Sometimes it's harder to find the setup than to let your funny little mind come up with a punchline.

My all time favorite activity is to watch stand-up comedy. Sometimes I just watch it for fun, but most of the time, without even trying, I am dissecting their punchlines in my head. I'm always asking myself, "Why did that work?" "Why didn't that work?" "What could've made that better?" "Does this remind me of anything I've done that I could setup similarly?"

Taking time to work through these exercises will not make you a funnier person; however, it will draw out of you the kind of funny thoughts that you have always had. Making people laugh is a gift, and when you are spending time writing humorous material you are investing time into learning how to share what will someday be an amazing gift for someone else.

A Final Note on Discipline

Discipline is the ability to make yourself do things you don't feel like doing. A Discipline is the process of breaking the abstract down into manageable pieces. In regards to humor, I have taken care of the latter one for you; you must take care of the first part.

We all need discipline because we get better through struggle, and let's face it, no one ever feels like struggling. Managing this dynamic tension is the difference between successful people who get what they want and unsuccessful people who take what they can get. Discipline is the difference between people who get no laughs and those who get to know laughs.

I promise you that you have "funny" in you. The question is, "Do you have the discipline to use what you've just learned to bring it out?" I hope that you do. I promise that a book on how to make yourself do what you don't feel like doing is on the way.

The average child laughs 400 times a day. The average adult laughs only eight. I hope this book has made you laugh a few times, but more important, I hope it becomes one of your greatest tools for bringing something we need into this world—more laughter.

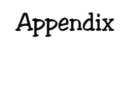

Appendix

Appendix A - The Funny Twenty for the Cycle of the Sale!

Prospecting

1. <u>Desperation Voicemail</u> -
★ "You're tough to get a hold of; you must be working too hard...want to trade jobs?"

2. <u>Improve Your Approachability</u> -
★ Wear outrageous clothing at a networking event such as a tie or shoes. This makes you more approachable and more memorable. It also releases the tension when you first meet someone.

3. <u>Use Funny Mailers</u> (from Gary Michels):
★ Instant Goodies - Send a package of instant oatmeal, instant coffee, instant pudding, instant mashed potatoes and Minute Maid Orange juice with a note: "By using these products hopefully you will find a few extra minutes in your crazy schedule to give me a call."

★ Crumpled Brochure - Send your marketing piece to them crumpled up with a sticky note on it that says, "Don't throw this away, AGAIN!"

★ Pizza Box - Send a pizza box with all your important information on it and a coupon for a free pizza inside and write "Gary Delivers" on the box.

★ Event Ticket - Send a ticket to a sporting event, theatre, or comedy club with a note that says "Doing business with me could be your golden ticket. I'll meet you there!"

★ Shot Glass - Take in a shot glass with your business card taped to it and write on the back "Give me a shot."

★ Needle In A Haystack - Send them a small cardboard box full of hay with one end of a string taped to the top and the other end attached to a needle with a note that says "Finding a good Realtor can be like finding a needle in a haystack. I'd love to help you!"

Initial Contact

4. Funny answering machine -
★ Write a jingle such as Kevin Vaden's: "You've reached the box now do the talks, you know just what to do. So leave your name the date and time, and your phone number too. And pretty soon when I return, I'll call you back, you'll see. Instead of this taped silliness, you'll be talking to me. Yeah."

★ "I'm either out of the office, away from my desk, or bungee jumping with the Dalai Lama..."

5. <u>Meeting someone for the first time</u> -
★ If they have a nametag on - "Hi, what's your name (nametag)?"

★ Tell them your name is an opposite gender name. For example a big guy could introduce himself as "Priscilla" or a soft spoken woman could introduce herself as "Frank."

6. <u>Business to Business Approach</u> -
★ "Hi my name is Rory and I'm not interested...oh wait, that's your line."

Qualifying

7. <u>Funny meeting times</u> -
★ "Can we meet from 11:31 - 1:17?"

8. <u>Business Lunch</u> -
★ "My name's Rachel, I'll be your server." "Oh, my name's Rory and I'll be your customer."

★ "What would you like to drink?" "The way things are going; can I get a Gatorade barrel of Vodka?"

★ "What would you like to eat?" "What's the worst thing on the menu?"

Closing

9. <u>Funny Number Price</u> -
★ "The house is 1.2 million dollars...and 27 cents."

10. <u>Handling Bargainers</u> (from Darren LaCroix) -
★ "What's your best price?" (Quote a number much more than normal price) When they say "That's not your best price" say "It is for me."

★ When someone makes you an offer just laugh. If you hold strong here they will often raise their price.

11. <u>Cash Collection Finisher</u> -
★ "We take cash, checks, credit cards...dogs, cats, and kids."

★ "We take all major credit cards...except Chevron, and Enron."

★ "We take cash...with two forms of ID."

Answering Objections

12. <u>"I'm busy"</u> -
★ "Oh, I'm sorry I didn't catch you cleaning out the gutters did I?"

13. <u>"I can't afford this."</u> -
★ "Well, if you could, would you pay with cash or credit card?"

14. If someone is frustrated -
★ "Who's winning today, you or the Computer?" (Whatever is causing the stress)

Referrals

15. Business Card Back -
★ "My goal is to provide a level of service that makes it very comfortable for you to sick me on your friends□."

Laughing Up The Office Environment

16. Funny Names List -
★ Keep a list by your desk of all the funny names of prospects you have called on.

17. Funny Signs -
★ Admin Sign: "All questions cost $1. If I have to think about it $5. A correct answer $20."
★ Bikram Yoga Studio: "Look better naked. Join Bikram."
★ Health Club: "Are you fat and ugly? Would you rather just be ugly?"

18. Funny Outing -
★ Have an office party at a local comedy club. They often have very good deals for this.

19. Funny Policies -
★ Hire a comedian to add humor to your company policies.

20. Theme Days -
★ Have theme days or dress up days around the office. This gets people thinking and causes new synapses to fire in their brain.

Reading List

As for the reading list, here it is...

Laugh and Get Rich - Darren LaCroix

Stand Up Comedy - Judy Carter

Comedy Writing Step by Step - Gene Perret

Punchlines, Pitfalls, and Powerful Programs - Scott Friedman

Punchline Your Bottom Line - David Glickman

Comedy Writing Secrets - Melvin Hellitzer

About The Author

Rory Vaden was raised for most of his young life in Boulder, CO by a struggling single mother and his older brother Randy. Encouraged by an incredible spirit of love from his mother Tessie and a healthy dose of discipline from his much larger brother Rory began to find success at a very young age.

He received his first degree black belt in Shao-Lin Kung Fu at the age of 10. It was here that Rory met a man named Kevin who he eventually recruited to take on the title of "Dad." Kevin and Tessie were married in 1992 and Kevin adopted Rory shortly after.

Supported by an unshakeable network of friends and teachers, Rory became Valedictorian on his way to receiving a full academic scholarship to The University of Denver. While at DU Rory was approached by a young girl named Tracey who introduced him to The Southwestern Company.

Over the next four years, Rory worked with The Southwestern Company recruiting small armies of college students to leave their homes in the summer to go out and sell educational children's books 80 hours a week door-to-door. It was the exemplary leaders at Southwestern that taught Rory the true principles of leadership and salesmanship.

At Southwestern Rory heard a speaker named Eric Chester. Eric's message so inspired Rory that he approached Eric and shared his lifetime dream of becoming a motivational speaker. Eric eventually took Rory under his wing and began mentoring him on what it took to become one of the best speakers in the world. After graduating Magna Cum Laude and going on to get his MBA, Rory set out to become the youngest World Champion of Public Speaking in history—a goal in which he fell short of by finishing in the top ten out of 25,000 contestants for Toastmasters International in 2006.

At that time Rory teamed up with two gentleman who had equally successful track records, Gary Michels and Dustin Hillis to begin Success Starts Now!™ The company quickly became one of the premier sales training companies in the world by sharing the proven principles of the 150 year old Southwestern Company. Rory dreams of continuing to impact people's lives through the stage but also has a strong passion for comedy and hopes to eventually do work in television and movies.

He believes that his gifts were not given to him so as to elevate the value of his name, but so that he can inspire people to follow his example of trying to lead a Christ-like life. He will spend his life recruiting and training as he hopes to exemplify The Southwestern Company's mission statement that "We build people and people build companies." Rory is convinced that he is nothing more than a fiduciary of the skills that have been given to him and a conduit for God's message to pass.

"Remember... be funny to make more money!"

Get In, Get Out, Get Rich!

Check bookstores everywhere or order here.
Toll-Free: 1-877-589-0606 ext. 704
seeured online ordering
www.ssnseminars.com

	#	@ 19.95 ea.
Gettin' In & Gettin' Out How to Get In Every Prospect's Door and Get Out with a Sale **Gary Michels** 204 pages $19.95 ISBN: 0-87197-529-7		
	Shipping	
	Order Total	

Shipping:
USA: $4.95 for first item; add $2.00 for each additional book

Please Print

Name _____

Company_____

Ship Too_____

City/State/Zip_____ Country _____

Phone _____ Email (optional) _____

Success Starts Now! ™
2451 Atrium Way
Nashville, TN 37214
phone: 877-589-0606 ext 704
fax: 615-884-3370
www.ssnseminars.com

MasterCard VISA AMERICAN EXPRESS DISCOVER

credit card # _____ expires:_____

please sign _____

No Laughs
to Know Laughs

Check bookstores everywhere or order here.
Toll-Free: 1-877-589-0606 ext. 704
secured online ordering
www.ssnseminars.com

No Laughs to Know Laughs	#	@ 14.95 ea.
How to be Funny To Make Money		
Rory Vaden		
112 pages $14.95 ISBN: 978-0-87197-535-5	**Shipping**	
	Order Total	

Shipping:
USA: $4.95 for first item; add $2.00 for each additional book

Please Print

Name _____

Company _____

Ship To _____

City/State/Zip _____ Country _____

Phone _____ Email (optional) _____

***Success Starts Now!*™**
2451 Atrium Way
Nashville, TN 37214
phone: 877-589-0606 ext 704
fax: 615-884-3370
www.ssnseminars.com

credit card #_____ expires: _____

please sign _____